KASPAR HAUSER

THE HOLY FOOL & THE PATH OF SACRIFICE

PAINTINGS

& SCULPTURE by GREG TRICKER

TEXT by JOHANNES STEUCK

FOREWORD by JONATHAN STEDALL

MILLWHEEL ART PRESS

MILLWHEEL ART PRESS

Gloucestershire Tel: 01453 834975

Copyright © 2006 Greg Tricker
The Cottage, Millbottom, Nailsworth
Gloucestershire GL6 0LA

The stories which complement each of the plates were collated by Greg Tricker with reference to the original source material in the bibliography

Book designed with illustrated drop caps and friezes by Greg Tricker

ISBN 0-9542873-1-2

'Artists can do something more:
They can vanquish the lie.'

ALEXANDER SOLZHENITSYN

CONTENTS

LIST OF PLATES 8

FOREWORD BY JONATHAN STEDALL 10

VERSE BY KASPAR HAUSER 12

KASPAR HAUSER—TEXT BY JOHANNES STEUCK 15

THE PLATES 37

APPENDIX TO THE PAINTINGS 136

BIBLIOGRAPHY 141

GENEALOGICAL TABLE 142

LIST OF PLATES

THE PRISON 39

THE WATER OF LIFE 41

MY LIFE 43

MY LIFE (DETAIL) 45

KASPAR AND THE LIONS 47

KASPAR AND THE HORSE (STONE) 49

THE HORSES 51

THE MYSTERY OF KASPAR HAUSER 53

MY FRIEND 55

I WANT TO BE A RIDER LIKE MY FATHER 57

KASPAR WRITES 59

RELEASED 61

KASPAR APPEARS IN NUREMBERG 63

THEATRE OF THE WORLD 65

THEATRE OF THE WORLD (DETAIL) 67

THE STABLE NOTE 69

THE TOWER 71

THE SOLDIERS 73

THE RED APPLES 75

THE PARADISE GARDEN 77

THE CLOCK MENDER 79

THE MIRROR 81

KASPAR READS LATIN 83

THE BLACKBIRD 85

The Circus Life 87

The Little People 89

Kaspar's Diary 91

Kaspar and Clara 93

Kaspar and the Angels 95

The Holy Fool 97

Kaspar's Dream and The Fountain 99

Kaspar's Dream and The Closed Doors 101

Kaspar's Dream and The Closed Doors (Detail)..... 103

Path of The Cross 105

The Path of Sacrifice 107

The Lavender Bag 109

Kaspar Crawls in the Snow 111

Murderers 113

Murderers (Detail) 115

Kaspar Jonah 117

The Saving of Kaspar Hauser 119

The Passing of Kaspar Hauser 121

The Ark Bearer 123

Moses, Kaspar and The Tablets 125

Moses, Kaspar and The Tablets (detail) 127

The Passing Over 129

The Kingdom of Kaspar Hauser 131

The Kingdom of Kaspar Hauser (detail) 133

FOREWORD BY JONATHAN STEDALL

THERE are so many things to say and to ask about Kaspar Hauser's short and extraordinary life. Who was he really, and why had he been treated so inhumanely as a child—excluded from all human contact? What I find almost more interesting and significant than anything else is the fact that such an obviously noble being could emerge from so bleak, dark and silent a background.

If, however, each one of us is born not as a tabula rasa—a clean slate, but rather comes into the world with a biography already, then the story takes on a new dimension—as does the story of every human being. William Wordsworth described the incarnating child as 'trailing clouds of glory'. In Eastern traditions this would be called karma; and there it is recognized that much of the baggage we bring with us is often far from glorious! Kaspar's baggage had a radiance that touches us still, so beautifully conveyed by Greg Tricker's paintings. He was, it seems, in that long and fine tradition of the Holy Fool. The word 'fool', however, could be misleading. To have displayed such outstanding qualities of purity and innocence during the few years he spent among people, in spite of his thwarted childhood, seems to indicate someone of extraordinary strength and spiritual maturity. It is a triumph of the human spirit which I believe is repeated in more modest ways day after day, year by year, all over the world. The simple goodness and courage that is displayed by countless people whose lives have got off to appalling starts is truly amazing.

It is not difficult to understand why Kaspar Hauser is one of the icons of the Camphill movement. Over the years I have filmed many aspects of their work for children and adults with special needs, and have been deeply touched by what comes shining through those damaged minds and bodies. Their vulnerability and their lack of guile allow one to glimpse what we all tend to conceal behind the various masks we wear. In this sense their tragedy, their suffering—like that of Kaspar Hauser, can be seen as a certain sort of sacrifice, for it is their presence in the world that helps to remind us that cleverness and appearances are not everything.

The German medieval mystic, Johannes Tauler, warned of the Herod in the world who wants to destroy the child in us—all that is pure and holy in our heart of hearts. The parents of Jesus were able to escape with their child, though the force that is Herod finally caught up with him. No one in the end was strong enough to protect the young Kaspar Hauser either. But the fact that such spirits live among us at all is, I believe, of profound importance—whether we acknowledge it or not. Nothing is wasted; nothing in vain. Our world is enriched by their presence, however short their stay. In his gospel, St John the Divine testifies so simply and so powerfully to this great truth and to our frequent inability to recognize it—'He was in the world, and the world was made by him, and the world knew him not'.

Humanity will be slowly transformed, I sense, to the extent that each human being is true to their divine nature and to their potentiality. The individuality whom we know as Kaspar Hauser was prevented from fully exploring and living out his own destiny in that one particular incarnation, but we benefited nonetheless in ways that are impossible to quantify or analyse. The visionary painter Cecil Collins once wrote:

> "I believe that there is in life, and in the human psyche, a certain quality, an inviolate eternal innocence, and this quality I call the Fool ... The Saint, the artist, the poet, and the Fool, are one. They are the eternal virginity of spirit, which in the dark winter of the world, continually proclaims the existence of a new life, gives faithful promise of the spring of an invisible Kingdom, and the coming of Light".

Herod may win many battles, but not the victory. The Holy Fool triumphs, I believe, because purity and love are the source of all life; evil is merely an aberration, albeit a very real and dangerous one.

Contentment is the greatest grace,
Contentment changes water into wine,
Grains of sand into pearls,
Raindrops into balsam,
Poverty into riches,
The smallest into the largest,
The most common into the purest,
The earth into paradise.

Beautiful is the heart which remains in harmony with itself at all times.
Beautiful is life itself as all deeds balance each other.

Kaspar Hauser

KASPAR HAUSER
A LIFE OBSCURED

TEXT BY JOHANNES STEUCK

"HERE LIES KASPAR HAUSER, RIDDLE OF HIS TIME,
UNKNOWN BIRTH, MYSTERIOUS DEATH, 1833"

THESE are the words inscribed on Kaspar Hauser's gravestone in Ansbach. His extraordinary appearance, short life and brutal murder still resonate to us almost two centuries later. Who was Kaspar Hauser? Where did he come from? What was the meaning of his life? What did he achieve? What might have happened if he had lived? Why was he killed? To begin to answer these questions we need to build a bridge. A bridge across deep, dark waters, to a place that can only be reached through faith, creative imagination and intuition. The inscription on his gravestone is a challenge, not only to solve a historical mystery but to explore the nature of the forces that battle for supremacy in the world and to open our hearts and minds to all that is good, childlike and uncorrupted in human nature.

The name Kaspar Hauser itself perhaps holds a clue. Kaspar is the name of the Green King, the one who brings Myrrh to the Jesus child.

Kaspar is also a fool's name, a jester, clown, simpleton, a person whose relationship to the world is not sober, practical or useful. 'Hauser' has an almost ironic ring to it: for Kaspar was essentially rootless, cut adrift from his past, passed from home to home, from house to house. Yet in the final analysis he did perhaps build a 'House', not with bricks and mortar, but a house of the spirit, a community for all truly seeking souls.

HISTORICAL BACKGROUND

T THE TIME of Kaspar Hauser's birth in 1812, Europe was still struggling with the backwash of the 'Enlightenment'. The Enlightenment which had been the great achievement of the 18th century. A sharp, cold, clear wind that reverberated through the dusty cobwebbed halls of European civilisation. The Enlightenment that promised to free mankind from tradition, inherited superiority and consigned all religious practice to the dustbin of superstition. The Enlightenment that celebrated the 'Rational' as the ultimate achievement of civilised man.

This lofty goal, bringing with it the ideal of equality and human rights, overstepped itself in the French Revolution and led ultimately to the 'Terror' and the Guillotine. The 'Rational' separated itself from all those other essential human qualities, compassion, devotion and love. Thus the machinery of the guillotine became in itself a symbol of the victory of the head over the body. For thought, separated from all that is living, leads to a 'severed head' and to death.

In 1799 Napoleon Bonaparte, brilliant general and son of a minor Corsican aristocrat, swept to power. After defeating all the European powers opposed to the benefits of the Revolution, like a second Alexander he strove to unite Europe by military force. It was perhaps his destiny to unite Europe but not through force of arms. In many ways Napoleon was not the monster portrayed in English history books; there was much good in him. In retrospect, a strong politically and economically united Europe might have avoided future wars. This strong, united Europe was absolutely rejected by the British who wished to dominate the world, the Prussians who were awakening to the idea of the 'Fatherland', and the Russians who had their own imperial designs. Napoleon died in exile in 1821 on the tiny island of St. Helena.

Romanticism created a counter-force, set itself against a purely rational solution to life's mysteries. The Romantics saw themselves as frail and paltry compared to the elemental force of nature. This never to be understood primal God/force existed in nature but also in the emotional and instinctual nature of human beings.

The greatest Romantics also celebrated something else, the enduring goodness of the human Spirit. To put this era into context, let me present a 'menu' of names: John Keats 1795–1821;

Lord Byron 1788–1824; Coleridge 1772–1834; William Wordsworth 1770–1850; Caspar David Friedrich 1774–1840; Eugene Delacroix 1798–1863; William Turner 1775–1851; Johann Wolfgang von Goethe 1749–1832; Franz Schubert 1797–1828; Ludwig von Beethoven 1770–1827; Samuel Palmer 1805–1881 to cite but a few.

William Blake (1757–1827) touched on a deeper mystical level of existence. In his Songs of Innocence (1789) he expresses a profound veneration of all that is childlike, innocent and unspoilt. In many ways Blake was a lonely prophet and herald of precisely those qualities that Kaspar Hauser embodied. His poem The Lamb is a fine example:

THE LAMB

Little Lamb who made thee
Dost thou know who made thee
Gave thee life and bid thee feed,
By the stream and o'er the mead;
Gave thee clothing of delight,
Softest clothing woolly bright;
Gave thee such a tender voice,
Making all the vales rejoice;

Little Lamb who made thee
Dost thou know who made thee

Little Lamb I'll tell thee,
Little Lamb I'll tell thee:
He is called by thy name
For He calls himself a Lamb;
He is meek and He is mild,
He became a little child;
I a child and thou a Lamb,
We are called by his name;

Little Lamb God bless thee
Little Lamb God bless thee.

ENEATH the scenes, in an historical subworld as it were, secret Brotherhoods were active. There has always existed a kind of threefoldness in these occult movements. Though very different in their seeming polarization, those to the left and those to the right had one fundamental thing in common: an absolute opposition to the legitimacy of the developing 'free' individual. This awakening of the individual to his freely undertaken task of love within the cosmos is the meaning of Christ's Death and Resurrection. Thus, by battling against true freedom, these secret Brotherhoods battle against Christ Himself. In the middle, holding the balance, were the Rosicrucians. They sought to reconcile the physical with the spiritual, to transform the very nature of substance, to spiritualise and to heal.

A T the time of the French Revolution, the great Rosicrucian master, the Comte de Saint Germain had appeared. He tried to guide the ideals—Liberty, Equality and Fraternity to a wholesome realisation, but the savage counterforces were too powerful.

In the lifetime of Kaspar Hauser, Germany was still a mosaic patchwork of little kingdoms and principalities. Each was independent, ruled by hereditary sovereigns who in their little worlds had absolute power.

In 1871, through external pressure from the French and an internal sense of growing nationalism, Germany was united under William I, who became the Prussian Hohenzollern Emperor. Nationalism is an inevitable development in the evolution of human consciousness, a progression from family, tribe to nation, but the means by which it is achieved and its expression can either be entirely negative or a force for the good. There was something very militaristic and brassy about the new Germany; Otto von Bismark its architect was both perceptive and bullying. Somehow the rich flowering of culture that had evolved in middle Europe through its writers, poets, philosophers, composers and painters was superseded by the boom of cannons and the rattling of swords.

In 1848, according to the historian Karl Heyer, many of the spiritual and social conditions were present for a quite different German development. The players were all there, but somehow a decisive personality was missing, somebody who in a sensitive and perceptive way could have linked the sparring princelings together.

There are strong indications that this personality was Kaspar Hauser, who by his absence created a kind of black hole, a tear in the fabric of the cloth of history. He would have been in his prime in 1848 and could perhaps have poured 'Content' into the 'Form' that his step-grandfather, Napoleon, should have created. A kind of new 'Castle of the Grail' could have been established, presided over by a new type of Initiate/King, of which Kaspar would have been the first.

I N C.S.Lewis' Narnia books, Aslan the Christ/lion is forever telling the children that "no-one is ever told what would have happened". In other words we should not burden ourselves with regret and wishful thinking, but live in the present and accept the adventure that offers itself.

Yet in the light of subsequent German developments, it is perhaps necessary to reject a completely inevitable view of history. We could at least consider the Great War, the Second World War and its aftermath, Hitler (who came to power exactly a hundred years after the death of Kaspar Hauser) and the third Reich as a kind of aberration, a Frankenstein monster. In this sense great historical sweeps are no different from an individual human biography. It is useless to be crushed by a sense of failure, by the endless nagging voices of missed opportunity and inappropriate action. Yet we should not be blind to all that might have been, should look it squarely in the face and pray for courage to continue.

The great Rosicrucian task of redemption, transformation and healing has become ever more urgent. And just as the good can be thwarted and corrupted, evil can be transformed and redeemed. By empathising with the life, suffering and death of Kaspar Hauser we can participate in this task, begin to make it our own.

Kaspar Hauser Enters Nuremberg

ASPAR HAUSER stumbled out onto the streets of Nuremberg on a Whit Monday morning in 1828. Whitsun or Pentecost is the festival of the Holy Spirit, when tongues of flame alighted on the heads of Christ's apostles. This pouring out of the spirit did not result in ecstatic babbling, but was a kind of inverse of the Tower of Babel. Human language which had differentiated itself into many tongues could once again be transmitted from heart to heart. The assembled masses experienced the 'truth' within themselves, thousands were converted to Christianity.

Kaspar's appearance kindled a flame in many hearts; as if by magic people were drawn to him. Yet where there are bright flames, there is also darkness and where there is purity and innocence, there is also deliberate confusion and corruption.

The shambling, incoherent boy, with his mish-mash of ill-fitting clothes, bleeding feet and ever-repeated message, "I would like to become a horseman as my father was", was promptly clapped into the local lockup, a tower. He had appeared clutching a strange enigmatic letter addressed to a certain Captain Wessenig, a Cavalry Officer. The unsigned letter read:

> *"I am sending you a boy, Captain, who wishes to become a soldier and serve his King faithfully. The boy was brought to me in 1815; one winter night he was suddenly found lying at my door. I have children myself, am poor, I can hardly make both ends meet; he's a foundling and I have not been able to ascertain his mother. I have never let him out of the house, no-one knows about him; he does not know the name of my house, nor does he know the village. You may ask him but he won't be able to tell you, for he's not able to talk decently. If he had parents—which he hasn't—he might have entered a decent calling; you need only show him anything and he will be able to do it at once. I took him out of the house in the middle of the night and he has no money about him, so if you don't want to keep him you will have to kill him and hang him up the chimney."*

THUS KASPAR passed from a secretive confinement to an open imprisonment in the Tower of Nuremberg. The prison warden, Hiltel, was in many respects the exact opposite of the unknown letter writer. His work gave him the opportunity to observe hundreds of people. He had first hand experience of every form of criminality, every twist and turn of abhorrent human nature and yet, despite his rude contact with 'fallen humanity', he had a 'seeing heart'. Uneducated, very much a man of the people, Hiltel recognised the essential goodness of Kaspar and stood by him to the very end of his life. In a conversation that he had with Professor Daumer, he asserted

> *"...Hauser was a pure child to begin with, even less than a child. To fraudulently misrepresent such a phenomenon is beyond human capacity, his innocence is so potent that he* (Hiltel) *would be forced to bear witness to it even if God himself were to assert the opposite."*

Kaspar was medically examined by the Nuremberg State Medical Officer, Dr. Preu, who had a trained scientific mind. Preu came to the conclusion that Kaspar was neither mad nor a trickster and noticed some interesting physical anomalies about the boy:

> *"Both knees evince an unusual formation. The ends of the femur and tibia at the joint bend over steeply at the back and are sunk in deeply at the front together with the patella; thus when Hauser sits stretched out on the floor with his feet level with the hollow of the knee there is no room for a piece of paper to be inserted between, though with most people a whole fist would fit in."*

A few days after his appearance in Nuremberg he was visited by Georg Friedrich Daumer, a 28 year old professor at the gymnasium. Destiny or good fortune had placed one man into a position to assist Kaspar, to be both midwife and hierophant at his 'birth'. Rudolf Steiner said of him that "it was impossible to value him too highly," and that Daumer was "the last Rosicrucian."

In Kaspar, Daumer recognised his life's work. He saw in him a being without a past, an angelic, childlike nature, whose feelings were uncorrupted and whose refined senses channelled impressions directly to a mind uncomplicated by wants and needs and ambitions. Daumer saw it as his task to educate this boy and bring him to maturity without spoiling his purity.

Through many halting conversations Daumer was able to discover certain things about Kaspar's past. He had been, for an immeasurable time, in a small underground room. When it was twilight he was awake, when it was dark he slept. He lay on the floor with his legs stretched out straight in front of him. He was chained to a bed and had two little wooden horses and a toy dog. When his bread came mysteriously in the morning, he offered morsels of it to his companions. This bread and the fresh water that also appeared daily, were his only fare.

SOMETIMES he would fall into a very deep sleep and when he awoke, he was washed, his hair and nails clipped and his bedding changed. He had never seen the light of the moon or sun or stars, had never felt the rain on his face and never met a single human being.

Then suddenly everything changed: the man whom he called the 'thee' had appeared and spoken to him, had shown him how to write his name, 'Kaspar Hauser', and taught him a few words.

The man then carried him out of his cell, taught him to shuffle by supporting him pressed close to his chest and walking backwards. The 'thee' had then abandoned Kaspar in the streets of Nuremberg with a letter in his hand. Characteristically Kaspar hardly had a single word of reproach for the 'thee', the man who had incarcerated him. Yes he had been deprived of his life and the richness of his childhood, but he had been secure and certainly when he was first thrust out into the harsh world he had longed for that lost security. He imagined that he would 'learn' and then the 'thee' would come and take him home.

Mayor Binder, the then Mayor of Nuremberg, published an announcement, which on the one hand requested information from the public and on the other, described the foundling's unusual appearance, nature and probable imprisonment. This was an act of love, whereby he wanted to serve Kaspar, but it created a storm.

 HE legal authorities were angered because vital evidence had been disclosed and the general public swarmed to see this phenomenon; hundreds climbed the tower steps of the jail to view this wonder, this strange primitive troglodyte, this half-grown child, this angel, this impostor. For it was rumoured, and rightly so, that his skin was very fair and soft, almost translucent, showing the blue veins, that his hair had the sheen of some underground animal and that the soles of his feet were singularly uncallused like those of a young child who had not yet learned to walk; yet even more remarkable than his appearance was his behaviour.

He seemed intimidated by light and noise and smell, could only utter meaningless words and would eat only bread and drink only water. This seemed utterly unbelievable to the good citizens of Nuremberg who offered him a variety of delicacies, including alcohol. This was seen to have the most profound effect on Kaspar, even a tiny whiff of wine from a considerable distance would induce fainting.

Anselm Ritter Von Feuerbach, the President of the Court of Appeal in Ansbach, became a lifelong supporter of Kaspar and reported after a visit to his prison:

> *"Kaspar had decorated the walls as far as he could reach with sheets of pictures which were presents from many visitors. He stuck them on the walls afresh every morning with his saliva, which was as sticky as glue, and took them down again as soon as it grew dark, to lay them in a pile at his side.*
>
> *On the bench which was fixed to the wall all around the room was his bed in one corner, which consisted of a sack of straw with a pillow and a woollen blanket. The whole of the rest of the bench was packed with a multitude of different kinds of toys, with hundreds of lead soldiers, wooden dogs, ponies and other Nuremberg goods etc."*

 ND as Kaspar stood tentatively, gropingly on the threshold of his second birth, other deeply familiar images are evoked. The coming of the shepherds and the mocking of Christ appear strangely rolled into one. It is as if his appearance in the world, an event of deep significance, calls forth fated responses. These responses can either be conscious or fundamentally instinctive. Kaspar had to be welcomed into the world; his people had to lay their gifts at his feet, even though this may often only have been in the spirit of curiosity or mockery.

Feuerbach, when he visited him early on in his incarceration gives us a rare glimpse of Kaspar's state of mind. In 1831, three years later, he was able to question him about the apparent horror and disgust that he felt when looking out of the tower window:

"When I looked at the window it always seemed to me as if a shutter had been placed in front of my eyes upon which a decorator had splashed paint from various brushes in a chaotic array of white, blue, green, yellow and red. I was unable to recognise and distinguish the single objects as I now can. That was therefore quite horrible to look at. And at the same time I was afraid because I thought that someone had closed brightly chequered shutters so that I would not be able to look out into the open. It was only later during my walks in the open air, that I realised that what I had been looking at, at the time, was fields, houses and hills and that which appeared to me to be much larger than another object was really much smaller than it and that some large things were much smaller than I had observed them. Eventually I did not see the shutters any more."

This is an experience of the world as pure perception, a phenomenon uninterpreted by the intellect. The normal experience of the very young child who has, as yet, not grasped the world, who has no concept of space and distance or size, everything is two-dimensional and incomprehensible.

THE DAUMER FAMILY

RIEDRICH DAUMER took Kaspar into his house where he was surrounded by all the love and care that Daumer, his sister and his mother could offer him. Kaspar went through a kind of crisis in which he hovered between life and death. His senses and sensibilities had been so overloaded by the onslaughts of all the visitors in the tower that he had collapsed from nervous prostration.

The Daumers nursed him with loving attention so that after three days or so his health returned and he was like one reborn.

Daumer observed Kaspar closely and made a record of his extraordinary sensibilities and perceptions. His senses, unused for long years, were in a state of super-awareness. He was able to read text in pitch darkness, could memorise a hundred names or more, only ever having heard them once. He had an uncanny awareness of metals—small metallic objects could be hidden in a room and Kaspar would unfailingly be drawn to them, like a dog to a bone.

There was one incident particularly that stood out from those early days; a savage dog broke through the fence from the neighbours and rampaged around the garden. Kaspar was sitting outside on a bench and the dog, on becoming aware of him, approached humbly and licked his hand. It is said that on witnessing this scene, Daumer wept. It was like a window into paradise, when man in

22

perfect innocence had lived in peace with the animals, a time in which there had been neither fear nor hatred. Despite his awesome discoveries, Daumer guided Kaspar into an ever closer relationship to the earth. The process of normalisation inevitably involved the loss of Kaspar's powers. Thus one could say that Kaspar's sudden release into the unsuspecting world, his rapid and unmitigated bombardment with sense impressions and his acquisition of ordinary skills was like a kind of inverse initiation.

This gradual education and orientation into the world is described movingly in Jacob Wassermann's book, *Caspar Hauser: the Enigma of a Century.* Very young children have no concept of animate or inanimate, living and lifeless. At first Kaspar could not understand why the stone statue in the garden did not get tired or bored.

 ATURE in a continuous process of growth and decay was incomprehensible to Kaspar. He had only ever encountered things made by man; that something could have grown or evolved were unfathomable mysteries. He thought that at first leaves and grass had been cut out with scissors. When he grasped the idea of a living, growing life-filled nature, he was filled with awe. Here is a description from one of Kaspar's essays of his remarkable sensitivity to a flower:

> *"I went into Herr Haubenstricker's garden and found a flower which appealed to me very much. I looked at it for a long time; observing it carefully. Then I asked Herr Haubenstricker what kind of flower it was and his answer was 'an imperial crown'. The next morning I told the Professor that I had seen a very beautiful flower and I told him how it looked. The Professor said that I should bring one and I went into the garden and picked one. When I grasped it and wanted to pick it, I got the same feeling as I had from snakes which I had seen, I got a chill; after a while I became very hot; I had a headache for a full quarter of an hour and the hand in which I carried the flower and felt as if it were lame. This lasted five minutes. Before the headache went, I shuddered; then the sensations were gone, but for several hours I did not feel as well as at first. I felt very tired and that is how I felt with snakes as well."*

Later, Kaspar developed a very special relationship to flowers and learnt to do beautiful water-colour flower paintings. When Kaspar saw children for the first time, he marvelled saying, "such little people." He had no concept that he himself had once been little, had grown and matured and would one day be old.

The distinction between subject and object—between self and the world had also to be learnt —very young children refer to themselves in the third person. Kaspar, in this respect, was still a very young child. He only understood that he was being referred to when his name was used and would talk about himself as 'Kaspar'. The ego had not yet embedded itself fully. Kaspar had to be helped into a realisation of his unique and separate identity.

As he became more normal, and he was given a greater range of food including meat, his acute sensibilities waned, but something else occurred. With the anchoring of a continuous self, vague dream images began to arise. At first he had flipped between waking consciousness and deepest sleep without any transitionary modes of dream. Now, with his awakening self, his sleep became disturbed; haltingly he described it himself in the words:

> *"During the night the dark sits on a lamp and howls."*

 HESE were dreams of profound loss and longing of castle interiors, picture galleries, fountains and closed doors. Environments that in waking life he could certainly never have known. His being had existed in such a state of purity and sense deprivation, that his 'memories' could reach back to a time beyond the formation of rational thought, when for most people experience is consciously irretrievable. Kaspar describes one of these dreams:

"On the night of the 2nd April I had a dream as if in reality I had seen a man with a white cloth hanging around his body, with bare hands and feet and he had looked wonderfully beautiful. Then he stretched out his hand to me with something that looked like a garland. Then he said that I should take it; then I wanted to take it; then he replied in two weeks you must die. Then I replied, I do not want to die yet because I have not been on earth very long and did not take the garland—when he replied to me, so much the better. Then he stood for a while before me and as I did not take the garland, he walked backwards towards the table, I got up and as I approached, it had begun to shine wonderfully. Then I took it and went towards my bed—as I approached my bed it began to shine more and more strongly; then I said; I will die, then he was gone. I wanted to get into bed, then I woke up."

Anselm Ritter von Feuerbach focused his fiery energy into solving the mystery of Kaspar's birth and imprisonment. He was the greatest criminologist of his time, a man imbued by a sense of humanity and justice who successfully ended the use of torture as part of criminal investigations.

By addressing himself so wholeheartedly to Kaspar's cause, he sacrificed his very life, for when his deliberations, first sent in a secret memorandum to the widowed Queen Karoline of Bavaria, Kaspar's aunt, were made public, he died mysteriously. There is a not unjustified suspicion that he was poisoned. His investigations pointed to a dynastic crime, cleverly concealed and brutally executed.

Research has now irrevocably proved Feuerbach correct. There had indeed been a particularly heinous crime, elaborate and far-reaching which, to this day, certain interested parties are still trying to cover up.

KASPAR HAUSER'S LINEAGE

 ASPAR HAUSER was born on September 29th, Michaelmas Day in 1812 in Karlsruhe. This birth on the feast of St. Michael again extends the mere biography into something greater, beyond itself. If indeed Kaspar's mission was to have been the establishment of a new kind of kingship in Middle Europe, in which blood ties, race and creed were superseded by a higher form of community, then perhaps in very truth he was a messenger of Michael. The Archangel Michael is celebrated in Christian tradition, as the 'Heavenly Warrior' and the 'Weigher of Deeds' at the end of time. As the fighter against evil, he calls upon our conscience to stand firm and exercise clarity of judgement. This clarity of judgement should not lead to harshness and condemnation but an ever expanding empathy. The sense that we belong to the family of mankind and that no-one anywhere is far enough away for them not to be our brother. Though never christened, he was given the name Stephan and was the heir to the throne of the Zähringen dynasty, son of the reigning Grand Duke Karl of Baden and his wife Stephanie

24

de Beauharnais, daughter of Josephine, and adopted daughter of Napoleon (see genealogical table, page 142). The Grand Duke Karl and Stephanie had three perfectly healthy daughters (who went on to marry into various European royal houses) and two sons who all died mysteriously, leaving no heir to the throne.

The regular Zähringen dynasty died out in the male line and Leopold, the son of the Old Grand Duke of Baden, Karl Friedrich (Kaspar's grandfather) and his second wife, Luise Hochberg ascended the throne.

Kaspar, who in his infancy seemed to have been strong and vigorous, was exchanged shortly after his birth with a dead or dying child. The identity of this child has since been discovered by Fritz Klee who investigated the matter very thoroughly.

 MONG the servants of Luise Hochberg there was a family called the Blochmanns. The couple, who had nine children, seem to have suffered from some genetic or blood group defect because all the children died in infancy. All apparently except one, Kaspar Ernst Blochmann. His name had been entered in the Karlsruhe Protestant Death Register of 1833 as having died in Munich on the 27th November. What is extraordinary about this registration is that the Blochmann boy has been given the wrong Christian name. In the Protestant Parish Registry of the city of Munich the name appears as Ernst. This Ernst Blochmann was apparently a soldier. Further investigations proved that no such man had ever served in the Bavarian Army. An attempt had been made by those responsible for the crime to give the changeling's death legal status. Kaspar Hauser was murdered 17 days after the exchanged child supposedly died. It was probably hoped that through this elaborate manoeuvre anyone attempting to identify Kaspar Hauser as a Prince of the House of Baden, would be thrown off track. By constructing a fake life and death for the Blochmann child it would be very difficult to claim that there ever had been an exchange of boys and that the Crown Prince Stephan (Kaspar Hauser) had not really died in infancy. With the exchange of the two boys the mystery begins—why was not the infant Kaspar quietly put out of the way? Disposed of? Smothered? It is only when we add another dimension to the dynastic crime, perpetrated by Luise Hochberg, that a possible glimmer of light appears.

The infant Kaspar was well looked after, vaccinated, loved even and appears to have had a normal first two and half years or so. These first few years are vital in the development of a human being, for the three great gifts of walking, talking and thinking are bestowed on him. These are not so much natural achievements of human biology as faculties bestowed by the highest spiritual powers.

The people responsible for his subsequent imprisonment must have watched this development closely. But not with the joy and love of any parent or educator, but with the intent of drastically intervening at precisely the right moment, of arresting this natural unfolding of human potential and thrusting Kaspar Hauser into a kind of limbo where he could neither live nor die. Thus they waited till his ego had to a certain extent taken hold of his incarnation and then condemned him for some twelve years to a small low cage in which he could neither stand nor walk, never heard or saw another human being and was surrounded by perpetual twilight or darkness. Was this aspect of the crime known to the dynastic usurpers or did the perpetrators act independently for reasons of their own? This has a strange fairytale quality.

Snow White's step-mother commands the huntsman to take little Snow White into the dark forest and kill her and to bring back her liver as a token of his deed. The Huntsman has compassion and lets her run away and returns to the wicked Queen with the liver of a wild boar.

Did Luise Hochberg know about Kaspar's further existence after the exchange of the babies? We do not know. The perpetrators must have wished to 'spoil' his incarnation, to ruin, retard and subvert a being who had a high and noble destiny. This possibility throws the doors open to all kinds of unpleasant ideas that we would probably rather not think about. We can accept evil is sometimes committed in ignorance, for the seemingly convenient motives of power, glory or wealth, but to admit the principle of conscious evil, seems somehow very far-fetched. Yet it is precisely this denial of the possibility of evil as a force in the world, objective, potent and ever active that gives it its strength. In medieval times devils were known and named, even depicted in stained glass windows, were part of the body of the church. We laugh at these childish fantasies—but it is the devil who laughs at us.

 F it is possible for the three Magi, of the Matthew gospel, to have a prophetic vision of the birth of the Jesus child, might it not be equally possible for the savants of the left hand path to have a premonition of the birth of Kaspar? To see that in the incarnation of this child their hopes were dashed, their plans in vain? Let us at least be open to the possibility. In contrast to the diabolical mechanisms of his enemies, Kaspar manifested nothing but innocence and goodness.

It was in the month of August, 1829 (about a year and a half after his appearance) when on a beautiful clear summer evening Daumer let him see the starry sky. Kaspar's astonishment and delight went beyond all description. He could not possibly take his eyes away; again and again he returned from inside the house.

He straightaway took into his gaze definite groups of stars, distinguishing the lighter ones from those that were less light and also their different colours. He called out "this is the most beautiful thing I have seen in this world! Who has put the lights there, who is lighting them, who is quenching them?" When he was told that like the sun which he already knew, they are continuously shining but cannot be seen, he again asked who had placed them there, that they continuously burn. His joy turned to melancholy, his body shook and he cried and could not be comforted. At last he asked why the evil man who had kept him in prison had never shown him this beauty. Finally he said, "this man should be put in a room like this for a few days so that he would know how hard it was." Prior to this experience, Kaspar had never said a hard word against the man who had imprisoned him.

Kaspar's strange powers attracted wide-ranging interest and curiosity. Daumer invited a constant stream of sightseers and all kinds of astonishing experiments were performed. This second wave of the intelligentsia was like an inversion of the adoration of the Kings. They did not come to worship or to give their gifts, they came to ogle and to be titillated.

Towards the end of his time with Daumer, his fine sensibilities seem to have been thrown into disarray. Daumer very much regretted that he had introduced meat into Kaspar's diet; it was probably this sensory over-stimulation and perhaps a desperate need for privacy which made Kaspar untruthful. He began to tell lies; one suspects that this aspect of Kaspar was misunderstood and exaggerated by his educators, who tended to view it as moral failure, rather than a child seeking independence.

 IS thirst for knowledge was tremendous; like a dry sponge he soaked in the wet world. It was almost as if he was trying to make up for all the years of dullness by grabbing hold of knowledge with all his might. He had riding lessons with a Herr Rumpler and learnt with astonishing quickness. The little toy horse that he had fed when in captivity now became a living creature. One can imagine with what joy and a growing sense of freedom he rode about in the countryside.

The horse in fairytales is intimately connected with thinking—a thinking directed towards the earth. It is a symbol of the will guided by thought—think of all the great stories in which the hero achieves his goal on the back of some special and mighty steed.

HE ultimate image of this aspect of the horse is the Wooden Horse of Troy. Kaspar riding is truly a picture of him taking hold of the reins of his life —beginning perhaps to find his identity. Yet this was not to be. Rumours had begun to circulate that Kaspar was going to write an autobiography, a story of his life. Kaspar was a celebrity; he had not disappeared into the army or become a stable boy. He was beginning to remember, to learn and even perhaps to recognise his destiny. His tormentors could not allow this to happen, they risked all in a move to silence him.

In October 1829 an attempt was made on Kaspar's life. An unknown masked assassin took a swipe at him with a meat cleaver. Just as the blow was falling, Kaspar ducked (he was on the outside toilet at the time and stooped to pull up his trousers) and the blade aimed at his throat sliced his forehead instead.

Wassermann tells how Kaspar, like a wounded animal, crept into the cellar, a dark hole such as he knew and remembered as comforting. The wound was not deep but had far-reaching consequences. It shook Kaspar's confidence to the core and in a strange way justified his vague memories and the rumours that circulated that he was of royal birth, for indeed if he was the bastard son of some peasant, why bother to assassinate him? The attack also precipitated his removal from Daumer's household. The professor felt unable to guarantee his safety (Kaspar was also put under 24 hour police guard) and perhaps a slight disappointment and weariness with Kaspar had set in; his unusual gifts (except for his astonishing memory) were disappearing fast. In the words of Feuerbach:

> *"Now to look at Kaspar, he is one of the most lovable creatures, radiating goodness like no-one else, but otherwise he is not in any way special. He is not a genius, he has no special capacities. He is just an ordinary human being—except for his kindness, his goodness."*

KASPAR MEETS LORD STANHOPE

ASPAR was put under the guardianship of Gottlieb Freiherr von Tucher, an aristocrat; an upright and unwavering supporter. As a temporary measure, presumably until something better could be found, Kaspar was transferred to the Biberbach household on New Year's Day 1830. Biberbach seems to have been a typical busy, overstretched businessman, whose work took up most of his time and energy. His wife, Frau Biberbach, was a bored, highly-sexed social climber.

The two policemen who guarded him continuously and accompanied him on all his visits and outings, drew unfavourable attention to him, and seemed to bestow an exaggerated and absurd importance—the fool with the bodyguard. He was mocked and teased mercilessly.

Kaspar withdrew into himself more and more, only wishing to study; however this precious space that he so desperately needed was never granted to him. Frau Biberbach treated him at first like a possession—a curiosity to be bandied about, shown to her friends, a curious creature that would reflect well on her and thrust her into the much sought-after limelight. Kaspar retreated into silence and petty lies, something she flung into his face later in her letters of denunciation. But first she had other plans. She could have been a mother figure for Kaspar, a loving and affectionate confidant, instead she tried to seduce him. An absent husband, an hysterical nature that suffered from mood swings, sexual frustration (probably fed by the trashy romantic literature of the time) fed her appetite.

This interlude, like so many others in Kaspar's life, takes on a dimension beyond itself, becomes almost legend. One is reminded of the story of Joseph and Potiphar's wife, her attempted seduction and its consequences. Hell hath no fury as a woman spurned. Kaspar withdrew more and more and utterly rejected her approaches. The nineteen year old still lived in a state of innocence and was both shocked and confused by Frau Biberbach's intentions. She, on the other hand, became a bitter enemy, filled with nothing but hatred for him. On the 15th July 1830, it was seen as expedient to remove him from the chaotic and dark clutches of Frau Biberbach. His guardian, Gottlieb Freiherr von Tucher took him into his house.

Tucher wanted above all else to fit Kaspar for a normal life in the workaday world. He was neither interested in Kaspar's strange powers nor in his supposed royal birth. He saw it as his task to educate him in a rational, sober and practical manner. Order, discipline, punctuality were

28

stressed. He was a good man, but perhaps lacking in imagination and empathy. Kaspar took to this structured, somewhat austere life like a fish to water. He spent much time on his own and would devote himself completely to learning; where everything had been confusion, sensuality and darkness in the Biberbach household, life with von Tucher was quiet, modest and well-ordered.

 HIS sober and protective bubble however soon burst, when a person perhaps as enigmatic as Kaspar Hauser appeared on the scene. This strange character who strode onto the stage was the Englishman, Philip Henry 4th Earl Stanhope. He was born on 7th December 1781 in Chevening House in Kent. He came from a high-born family, from which many worthy and important individuals were descended. William Pitt, the Prime Minister, was an uncle. Wassermann, in his novel, paints a very telling picture. Stanhope was in many ways the antithesis of Kaspar. He too came from the 'upper echelons' but had been nurtured in an environment of privilege and wealth. He, spoke both French and German fluently and was richly endowed with all the faculties of nature and nurture. But, unlike Kaspar, who was essentially a being of innocence and love, Stanhope was a creature of experience who hankered for adulation.

Fifty at the time of their meeting, he was still handsome, elegant and stylish and apparently very wealthy. Strangely enough, Stanhope arrived in town four days after the assassination attempt on Kaspar. No-one was ever caught or questioned. This attack was in many ways a dress rehearsal for the actual murder, in which the murderer glided away effortlessly and unapprehended.

On the 28th May 1831, Stanhope met Kaspar for the first time. Seeing the effect of Stanhope's influence and subsequent betrayal, one is forced to assume that it had a single purpose: to seduce and corrupt this boy, to lead him astray so that the goodness and light could be extinguished and Kaspar's innocence, and moral integrity destroyed. Kaspar had emerged from his twelve year confinement miraculously un-stunted, still able to learn, radiating an innocence and purity that attracted countless people. The assassination attempt had failed by pure chance, now it was Stanhope's turn. Stanhope the needy, Stanhope the worldly, the impeccable actor, Stanhope the anti-Kaspar.

The 'rich' and 'affectionate' Earl made many promises, they would travel to foreign lands, he would take Kaspar to his castle in England, he would adopt him. He might even bring him to his mother and help to restore him to his throne. These extraordinary fantasies of course had a very devastating effect on the inexperienced and vulnerable soul of Kaspar, but probably more destructive than any broken promise was the illusion of unconditional love. To at last have met someone who seemed truly to be a friend who offered understanding and lifted him out of the loneliness of his life must have been infinitely reassuring.

 ONE of Stanhope's promises came to anything, they evaporated into thin air. But what he succeeded in doing was to undermine Gottlieb von Tucher's austere pedagogy and fill Kaspar's head with wild hopes and expectations. He successfully tore Kaspar away from his circle of friends and protectors in Nuremberg and got him transferred to the small town of Ansbach. Here there was nobody he could confide in except the President of the Appeal Court, Anselm von Feuerbach. Feuerbach had signed his own death warrant with his pamphlet, *'Kaspar Hauser; the example of a crime against the soul of a human being.'*

ASPAR was now placed under the guardianship of Stanhope, Tucher having relinquished his in face of the impossible task that confronted him. He went to live in the house of the Meyers, a teacher couple, and came under the police surveillance of Hickel. Thus Kaspar entered a kind of trinity of evil. Stanhope, who was betraying him; Meyer, who with mean-minded scepticism and pedantic, utterly unimaginative teaching, constructed a second prison; and Hickel, who in his capacity of Chief of Police should have been an upholder of justice, but was in actual fact in the pay of Kaspar's adversaries. He was obsequious and fawned on his superiors, showing a kind of narrow-minded, brutal stupidity that only an intelligent man can. Convinced that Kaspar was a swindler of the lowest kind, he made it his task to 'find him out'.

Meyer created a kind of microcosm of 19th Century Materialism, a prison of petty concepts and irrelevant information from which all life-giving creativity and joy had been rigorously excluded. For ultimately Stanhope had failed, his betrayals had neither broken nor corrupted Kaspar; Meyer's approach would be more insidious, more difficult to withstand, the slow, dull wearing away of a once high and noble mind.

When he was not being taught Latin, Grammar or Mathematics, he worked as a clerk in the court of appeal. Kaspar hated both his lessons and his mindless job. Yet even Meyer did not fully succeed.

Kaspar made two friendships with young women of noble birth because, although his enemies had hoped to plunge him into the obscurity of Ansbach, he was still sought after and invited to people's homes.

His widowed mother, Stephanie de Beauharnais, came secretly to Ansbach to see her supposed son. She could only gaze at him from a distance, fainted and had to be carried away by her waiting maids. What she felt and thought we can only imagine—to see her dead son Stephan after all these years, years in which she had lost two sons, a husband and become a virtual prisoner in her own home—must have been almost unbearably painful.

NE man shines out in this last lap of Kaspar's life, these two years spent in Ansbach; this is pastor Fuhrmann, the churchman who prepared him for his confirmation. He seems to have been a representative of true Christianity and remained true and faithful to the end. Kaspar was confirmed in the church of St. Gumbertus in Ansbach on May 20th 1833. This was a beautiful old church which had built into it a special chapel which belonged to the order of the Knights of the Swan. This order was founded on Michaelmas Day, September 29th 1440 by Fredrick II of Brandenburg. According to Rudolf Steiner, the Knights of the Swan were permeated by a true Grail stream which worked therapeutically on earth. Fuhrmann writes about the confirmation:

> "The 20th May of last year was the festive occasion of which hundreds still say it is a day of exaltation for them. It was the day of Kaspar Hauser's confirmation, the most respected families of the district, in whose hearts feelings of compassion were aroused for the pitiable young man, surrounded him and his guardians and advisers who accompanied him on his journey to the overcrowded chapel—our lovely Gumbertus Church. A prayer was sung in four parts by the choir. Prepare in me O Lord a heart that is pure and give to me a new and steadfast spirit, cast me from thy presence not aside, nor take thy Holy Ghost away from me.
> During the singing Hauser knelt on a prayer stool before the altar. The moment, however, when he knelt, the emotions with which he spoke

the above words in the silence had an unusual effect on the whole congregation. Every lip moved quietly in response; all hearts prayed with him and for him."

KASPAR'S LAST DAYS

 N December 14th 1833, which was a cold and foggy day, a stranger appeared at the court house. He promised to show Kaspar 'something', probably hinted that he would learn something about his mother. They went to the park, which was deserted, and by the memorial of Uz, an Ansbach poet, the man handed Kaspar a lavender pouch saying, "in there is the information that you need." As Kaspar was fumblingly trying to open it, the man stabbed him in the chest with a razor sharp stiletto.

Kaspar ran home by which time snow was blowing all around and showed the wound to Meyer, who unbelievably marched the mortally wounded boy back to the 'scene' of the crime. There on the ground was the lavender pouch which Meyer took and then marched Kaspar back to his house again. It was only after this terrible ordeal that he was allowed to go to bed. The doctor, when he eventually came, found that Kaspar's lung and liver had been pierced and that he only had a short time to live. Meyer, that great pedagogue, that paragon of learning, even now did not believe that Kaspar had been assaulted. He begged him to the very end to confess that he had 'tried to hurt himself a little' perhaps in a bid to attract attention. The lavender pouch contained a note written in mirror-writing which read:

> *"Hauser will be able to tell you exactly what I look like and where I come from. To save Hauser this effort, I will tell you myself where I come from. I come from .... on the Bavarian frontier, on the river .... I can even tell you my name, M.L.O."*

Pastor Fuhrmann came to comfort him and Kaspar said:

> *"Tell all whom I knew that I ask for forgiveness."*

He died with the words 'tired...tired' on his lips.

King Ludwig of Bavaria offered ten thousand florins for information about the murder, but no-one ever came forward with the tiniest scrap of evidence. Kaspar was buried on the 20th December 1833. Many people attended the funeral; again it was as if a strong magical current had flowed through the masses, alerting them that something momentous—indeed truly irrevocable was taking place. In Wassermann's novel the burial is given a kind of cosmic aspect. Both sun and moon are clearly visible in the sky, like a motif from some old painting of the Crucifixion, Good Friday and Christmas Eve fuse. The Innocent Child, instead of being reborn again in our hearts, is crucified and dies.

HE death of Kaspar Hauser intensified the struggle for a clear understanding of his identity. Enormous measures were undertaken by his enemies to besmirch his name: they instigated a campaign of slander, attempting to prove beyond a shadow of a doubt that he was a swindler and an impostor. Meyer stubbornly maintained that Kaspar's 'wound' had been self-inflicted—an act of attention-seeking self-harm that had gone too far. Meyer's son wrote a very clever book denouncing Kaspar. This book spurred the then elderly Daumer into action, inspiring him to write a number of books about Kaspar Hauser. In his last summative book, *Kaspar Hauser*, he gave the following dedicatory poem:

Life's pilgrimage will soon be done,
I feel my powers ebbing fast;
Yet once again, my poor child,
I see thy blood-drenched shadow rise.

Thy spirit lips they whisper soft:
O thou, my friend, however true.
My knight and my protector aye,
However hard the strife might be!

I was—that knowest thou full well—
Ne'er to gruesomeness disposed;
The one has struck me in the breast,
The others covered me with shame.

Thou strovest here, thou strovest there
The triumph of innocence answered
And in my dismal haven I
Slept once again in deepest peace.

But never rest the wiles of hell,
The rage of hell upon the earth;
After respite I am once more
Reviled and trodden underfoot.

Oh let me test thy love and courage
In the present battle too;
Take me under thy protection
From above strength shall not fail.

Thou speakest and I'm here at hand;
I and my sword serve as of old,
And sacred is the faithful bond,
Our duty now we shall perform.

All his friends, who had known him from the beginning, remained true to him. The prison warden Hiltel, Binder the Mayor, Herr von Tucher, all vouched for his innocence, purity and goodness.

Interestingly enough Lord Stanhope was particularly vociferous in his denunciations. He tried to gather 'statements' that would prove Kaspar's bad character, even going so far as to visit Daumer for this purpose. We can only guess at his exact relationship to the crime—who paid him and why; that he had no actual hand in the murder is clear. Stanhope drew attention to himself by attempting to deflect it. He was in Vienna at the time of the murder and had posted a letter to Kaspar Hauser from Munich on December 25th 1833. It is very unlikely that he would not have been aware of Kaspar's fatal wounding which occurred on the 14th, eleven days earlier. A memorial was placed near the Uz monument at the spot where Kaspar was stabbed. It read:

HIC OCCULTUS OCCULTO OCCISUS EST

There was secretly murdered one who was a mystery.

THE CHILD OF EUROPE

HE Child of Europe'—this title attached itself to Kaspar and perhaps defines more than any other the meaning of his life. He was an orphan, a foundling, mother and fatherless, he appeared in Nuremberg. Yet he embedded himself more firmly into the hearts and minds of people than many a son or daughter. Those qualities that he embodied—innocence, joy, wonder and love—have never been so under threat as they are today. Kaspar's short biography has now almost become a universal story. The demons of materialism seek to reach into the very womb itself to affect and manipulate the incarnating human being. The 'prison house', that drab, grey state imposed with such thoughtless intelligence on every child, has almost extinguished all creativity, all longing for the spirit. We have forgotten the sacred otherness of childhood, when all the world still seemed to shine with the light of Heaven.

The destruction of Kaspar Hauser was an attempt to destroy all that is good and gentle and innocent in our souls so that the great lie could be ever more loudly proclaimed—childhood is our fantasy of a bygone era, there never really was such a thing, it was only ever a sentimental construct, a privilege of the wealthy.

Yet deep down we know we are uneasy, buy things, drink things, take things to make the uneasiness go away. And all the time the uneasiness grows: we are infected by some deadly contagion that will not let us rest. The world is disintegrating all around us, we are drifting out into the dark, deep sea—surely there must be something we can do? How can innocence and joy, wonder and love be made to return to this stark world?

The great visionary poet and painter, Cecil Collins (1908–1989), who in many ways carried forward that precious baton of spirituality from William Blake, writes:

> "The crucifixion of the poetic imagination in man by the Machine Age is a religious fact. And modern society has succeeded very well in rendering poetic imagination, Art and Religion, the three magical representatives of life, an heresy and the living symbol of that heresy is the fool. The fool is the poetic imagination of life, as inexplicable as the essence of life itself. This poetic life, born in all human beings, lives in them while

34

they are children but is killed in them when they grow up by the abstract mechanisation of contemporary society and by the teaching of the 'ordinary man', 'the man in the street'."

"The greatest fool in history was Christ. This Great Fool was crucified by the commercial Pharisees, by the authority of the respectable, and by the mediocre official culture of the Philistines. And has not the church crucified Christ more deeply and subtly by its hypocrisy, than any pagan? This Divine Fool, whose immortal compassion and holy folly placed a light in the dark hands of the world."

Further:

"It is the element of the Fool in every man that can redeem him from Degradation, this ancient element of the eternal Adam still exists deep inside a man, the element in him that holds converse with the essence of life. Spiritual joy that is essential joy, arises from innocence, from purity of consciousness—this is the fool. The fool in man is a divine debonair spirit, whose careless empirical gaiety and overflowing mercy embraces life, but the fool is more than this, he is the sorrow of life. Where there is no reverence or respect for the creative impulse of Art and Religion, there can be no civilised society. Civilisation exists only where conscience exists. And conscience is individual; one individual with an awakened conscience towards life is civilisation, and where there are a thousand people without conscience, there is no civilisation."

Thus it is perhaps as 'The Divine Fool' that Kaspar Hauser can inspire us, give us strength and courage to find the art and poetry and religion within ourselves and toss it laughingly and unashamedly into the world.

Kaspar can also give us comfort, hope and courage when we are overcome by grief in contemplation of our own destiny; how imprisoned, stunted, thwarted and subverted our own life has run its course! And yet into whatever blind alley or folly we have lost ourselves there is yet hope. Hope that as long as we struggle and strive for that which is true and pure and good we never will be lost.

Karl König, the founder of the Camphill movement, connected it very intimately with the being of Kaspar Hauser. For König, Kaspar Hauser was a kind of patron saint for people with special needs. An embodiment of potential restricted by circumstance.

Jacob Wassermann, who was motivated by a profound love and intuitive understanding of Kaspar Hauser, wrote:

"He will be as mighty in death as he was powerless in life."

Rudolf Steiner ascribes to Kaspar Hauser the task of 'Bridge Builder'. The dense cloud of Materialism that enveloped humanity in the 19th century was such, that the connection between the spiritual and the physical was all but obscured. The sacrificial death of Kaspar Hauser opened a chink in the mirk, rays of spirit light could once again illuminate the minds and hearts of men.

By forgiving his murderers, Kaspar ceased to be a victim; imposed suffering and death became a deed of sacrifice. In an act of freedom he accepted his terrible fate and placed it into the service of Evolution, into the stream of light. Through forgiveness, he identified himself with a higher will; 'The Not I'—but the Christ in me.

It is thus as one 'crucified' and 'resurrected' that he could extend his hand to ailing humanity and like the snake in Goethe's fairytale—'The Green Snake and the Beautiful Lily' became the bridge over the abyss.

35

THE PLATES

THE PRISON

" THE *History of Kaspar Hauser I shall write myself..... The prison in which I was obliged to live until my release was about six to seven feet wide and five feet high...... at the front there were two small windows with wooden shutters which looked quite black.*"

Kaspar Hauser

Size 15½ x 14¾ inches
Oil on wood

THE WATER OF LIFE

" I very often took the little jug in my hand and held it to my mouth
for a long time but no more water ever came out of it. I put
it down again and again and waited for a while to see if water
would soon come, since I did not know that water had to be
brought to me, I had no idea that there could be anyone other
than me. When I waited a while and no water had come, I lay
on my back and fell asleep. I awoke again and my first reaction
was to reach for the bread and whenever I awoke there was water
in the jug and a loaf of bread there. I nearly always drank all
the water and then I felt very well."

Kaspar Hauser

Size 29¼ x 45¼ inches
Acrylic & tempera on wood

MY LIFE

"ON the floor there was straw on which I used to sit and sleep. My legs were covered from the knee with a rug. Next to my bed on the left there was a hole in the ground in which there was a pot; there was also a lid on it which I had to push aside and always covered it again. The clothes I wore in prison were a shirt, short trousers but without a seat since I could not remove them to use the pot......

..... I knew nothing of the human world and so long as I was locked up and had never seen a human being. I had two wooden horses and a dog, I always played with these, but I cannot say whether I played with them the whole day or not, since I did not know what a day was or a week."

Kaspar Hauser

Size 42 x 17¼ inches
Tempera & acrylic on wood

MY LIFE

Detail

KASPAR AND THE LIONS

Kaspar pure in heart and spirit, a Holy Fool,
is imprisoned like Daniel in the lions' den

Size 9 x 10 ¾ inches
Oil on Wood

KASPAR AND THE HORSE

Size 33 x 17 x 3 inches
Portland stone

THE HORSES

"THE braces were on my bare body and the shirt went over them.
My food was nothing but bread and water, I occasionally had too
little water but there was always enough bread. I had two horses and
a dog with which I always kept myself amused—I had red and blue
ribbons which I used to decorate the horses and the dog but sometimes
they fell down because I could not tie them. When I woke up the piece
of bread lay next to me and a little jug of water..."

Kaspar Hauser

Size 16 x 20 inches
Oil on canvas

The Mystery of Kaspar Hauser

Kaspar
Lost to the world,
Lost to himself.
On his own
In the play,
A Greek tragedy;
He reaches to his friend,
the little horse
To the spirit of life.

Size 46 x 29 ¾ inches
Tempera & acrylic on wood

MY FRIEND

Kaspar never saw the sky, sun, moon or stars,
his friend was the toy horse.

Size 16 x 12 inches
Oil on Canvas

I Want to be a Rider Like My Father

"I had the idea the horses had gone. I also had the thought when the horses come, I shall tell them not to go away again, and I wanted to say to them they should not let the bread go away, otherwise there won't be any for you."

Kaspar Hauser

Size 18 ½ x 23 ¾ inches
Tempera & acrylic on wood

KASPAR WRITES

ONCE *while Kaspar was awake, the wall opened and there stood a huge figure of a man. The ceiling seemed to rest upon his shoulders and he said aloud the word 'thee'. Kaspar always called his jailer 'thee' after that.*

The 'thee' put a bench with rounded feet in front of Kaspar and placed a piece of paper onto it. He helped direct Kaspar's hand to write his name, and also to remember various words; saying over and over again, 'learn, learn, learn'.

Kaspar scratched the letters of his name on the paper and it pleased him, as they were black and white.

Size 11½ x 9 inches
Gouache & wax on paper

RELEASED

THE *jailer awakened Kaspar during the night with difficulty and dressed him in trousers, a shirt and some large boots. He then lifted Kaspar onto his back and carried him up the stairs while Kaspar clasped his hands around the jailer's neck. It seemed to Kaspar as if they were climbing a large hill.*

Size 14 x 9 inches
Gouache & wax on paper

KASPAR APPEARS IN NUREMBERG

ON *Whit Monday 1828 Kaspar Hauser suddenly appeared in the Unschlitt Square. He was dressed like a peasant wearing an old frock coat, from which the skirts had been cut, a red tie and high leather boots. The first people whom he met were two shoemakers, as he came swaying down the street holding a letter. He could only walk slowly and painfully. Their attempts to come into conversation with him failed; but they managed to help him along the street to the riding master's house where Kaspar's letter directed them.*

Size 16 x 18 inches
Watercolour, wax & ink on paper

THEATRE OF THE WORLD

THE *curtains of the world theatre are drawn. Kaspar stumbles out onto the stage of life holding a letter; reaching for the sun. Death is masked and waiting. The people of the world look on in wonder.*

Size 41¾ x 48 inches
Acrylic & tempera on wood

Theatre Of The World

Detail

The Stable Note

WHEN *Kaspar arrived at the riding master's (von Wessenig) house with his letter, the owner was not at home. Kaspar was told to wait in the stables till he returned. He was offered beer and meat to eat which he refused with disgust, but he accepted bread and water willingly. Afterwards he fell asleep. When the riding master returned home, Kaspar was awakened with difficulty; he noticed the shining sword and bright uniform of the riding master and became fascinated, wanting to touch him admiringly. The riding master abruptly sent him to the Police Station.*

Size 32 ¾ x 17 ¾ inches
Tempera & acrylic on wood

THE TOWER

"WHEN I had been at the police station for a while, they led me to the tower. I had to climb up a very steep hill and cried because everything hurt so much. When I arrived at the tower, someone again spoke so loudly that I was in even more pain. I wept for a while and went to sleep. When I woke I sat up and wanted to reach for my water to quench the thirst I felt; I saw no water or bread, instead I saw the floor which looked quite different from the one in the place I stayed in before. I wanted to look around for my horses to play with them, but they weren't there either, so I said: I want to be a rider like my father too, by which I meant where are the horses and the water and the bread. Then I noticed the sack of straw on which I was sitting and looked at it in such astonishment and did not know what it could be. When I had looked at it for a very long time, I tapped it with my finger, whereupon I heard the same sound as that made by the straw in the place I stayed in before, on which I always sat and slept. I also saw many other things which filled me with such astonishment which cannot be described. I said: I want to be a rider like my father too, by which I meant: what is this, and where are the horses? I heard the clock strike again; I listened for a very long time; when I heard no more I saw the stove which was green in colour and gleamed."

Kaspar Hauser

Size 21¼ x 36¼ inches
Oil on wood

70

THE SOLDIERS

KASPAR *stayed in The Luginsland Tower on the 'Vestner Tore' where many people from Nuremberg continued to visit him, moved by compassion and curiosity. Kaspar had an extraordinary memory; he could recall, after having seen 70 or 80 visitors, all their names and occupations.*

Kaspar's room was small, clean and bright. He was dressed in a pair of long leg coverings, bare-footed and wearing a shirt. On the bench, which was fixed to a wall all around his room, was his bed in one corner. It consisted of a sack of straw with a pillow and a woollen blanket. The rest of the bench was covered with small toys, lead soldiers, coins and small ponies. These gifts were all packed away by him in the evening and then, as soon as he was awake, he unpacked them all and arranged them carefully and in order around the room.

Size 23 x 29 ½ inches
Acrylic & Tempera on Wood

THE RED APPLES

KASPAR *loved the colour red. He almost wished he could clothe himself and others from head to feet in deep red. He took no pleasure from the greens of nature that surrounded him. One day he saw a tree covered with red apples which delighted him, but he thought the tree would have been much better if the leaves had also been red.*

Size 17 ½ x 24 inches
Oil on Wood

THE PARADISE GARDEN

THERE *was a time when Kaspar could be seen in the garden, seated on a bench with a book in his hand. Swallows flew near him, doves pecked at his feet, and a butterfly rested on his shoulder. In him could be seen the Holy Fool in the Paradise Garden.*

Size 23 ¼ x 46 ½ inches
Acrylic & Tempera on Wood

THE CLOCK MENDER

DURING *some afternoons Kaspar would spend time alone. Next to his room was a small chamber which had been fitted up as a workshop. When he had completed his lessons he did all kinds of joinery and fine cardboard work, in which he became very skilful. The taking apart and putting together of clocks gave him great pleasure.*

Size 18 x 23 ¼ inches
Pastel and pencil on Wood

THE MIRROR

KASPAR *was deeply intrigued by a royal picture of Napoleon Bonaparte he had seen on a wall while he waited alone in a large reception room. He began to walk up and down the room majestically, as if the royal presence compelled him to imitation; and he began to sense something of his royal connection.*

On another occasion he was puzzled when he passed himself in front of a mirror, "Ah", he thought, a little troubled, "who is that?" He looked behind the mirror with curiosity, only to find there was no-one there.

Size 46 x 23 inches
Tempera & Acrylic on Wood

KASPAR READS LATIN

KASPAR *was ordered to study Latin grammar and exercises with words and phrases he could not fathom. This seemed like a second imprisonment to him, where he was shut off from nature in a dusty classroom. In despair he would say "I have no idea what I am going to do with all these Latin things, as I'm not going to be a parson, nor do I wish to become one." When his teacher told him that Latin was essential to learn the German language, his common sense answer was: "did the Romans have to learn German in order to speak Latin properly?"*

Size 24 x 36 inches
Tempera & Acrylic on Canvas

THE BLACKBIRD

KASPAR was taken into care by the half-mad Frau Biberbach who caused him much distress and unhappiness. On one occasion during a thunderstorm it seemed to Kaspar as if there was a big man outside scolding him. The blackbird, which sat in a cage near the window with a drooping head, at times made little piping sounds. He would have set it free long ago, for he pitied the bird, but he feared Frau Biberbach's scorn.

When the storm abated he quickly threw off his clothes, crept into bed and covered himself up to his forehead in order not to see the lightning. In his hurry he even forgot to lock the door and this circumstance had a curious sequel.

On the next morning when he awoke he noticed a penetrating smell. Yes, there was the smell of blood in the room. Shuddering, he looked about and the first thing he noticed was that the bird cage by the window was empty. Kaspar looked for the blackbird and perceived that it lay dead on the table, its wings spread out in a pool of blood, and next to it on a white plate lay the little bleeding heart.

What could this mean? Kaspar made a face and his mouth trembled like that of a child before it cries. He dressed to go to the kitchen to question the servants, but as he left the room he suddenly became frightened, for Frau Biberbach stood in the corridor next to the room. She had a broom in her hand and was decidedly untidy in appearance. Kaspar looked at her sallow face and continued to look at her for a time with almost the same dismay and feeling with which he had looked at the dead bird.

Size 44 x 48 inches
Acrylic & Tempera on Wood

THE CIRCUS LIFE

KASPAR *had been lodging for a while with the half-crazed woman Frau Biberbach. One day she waited for an opportunity when Kaspar was away from the house, and then had all of his possessions, clothes, underwear, books and other objects thrown into a box and carried into the street. Then she locked the door of the house and smiling with satisfaction, sat down at the balcony window on the first floor to watch for Kaspar to return and to enjoy the amazement of the assembled crowd. When Kaspar returned he leant against the box in the rain looking up in amazement at Frau Biberbach.*

Size 23 ¼ x 44 inches
Tempera & Acrylic on Wood

The Little People

AT times Kaspar would stand by the garden fence and look over into the next garden where children were playing. He would study their ways with amused interest. "Such little people," he would say, "such little people". His voice sounded sad and puzzled.

His friend Daumer explained to him that Kaspar had once been small and that he had grown bigger. To this he said: "Oh no, no, not Kaspar, Kaspar always like now, Kaspar never had such short arms and legs, oh no."

Kaspar found it hard to comprehend that things grow. When he was told that every living thing grows and that the trees in the garden were also alive and growing, he seemed a little disturbed as he listened to the rustling of the leaves on the trees. He looked dubious and asked, "Who has cut out all these leaves and why, why so many?" These too have grown, came the answer.

Size 15 ½ x 13 ½ inches
Gouache, Ink & Wax on Paper

KASPAR'S DIARY

K*ASPAR sat by the open window that looked over the garden until nightfall and enjoyed the silence. He struck a light and found his diary that he kept hidden behind an engraving on the wall.*

He sat at the table writing in his diary small incidents and joys of his daily life; and his history of his early beginnings as he remembered them. These thoughts were meant for his mother to whom the diary was dedicated. The thought that any other eye than hers should see them was inconceivable to Kaspar, although others tried to take the diary away from him.

On one occasion, after a dream, he made an intricate drawing of a face-like statue in his diary and added below the mysterious words:

> *Oh! Great One! Say! What wouldst thou have of me?*
> *Thou followest me, and followest a blind track.*
> *Beneath thy gaze my aspect is transformed:*
> *The dungeon doors are opened and the child*
> *That lay there long imprisoned issues forth.*
> *Gone are the mantle and the sword and the crown:*
> *And riderless the white horse rides afield.*

Size 22 ¼ x 16 inches
Gouache & tempera on canvas

90

KASPAR AND CLARA

A beautiful woman, Frau von Kannawurf, would often meet Kaspar to talk with him and to go for long walks together. She had a slight sing-song voice and was in the habit of blinking her eyelids when she spoke. She would wear her hat with ribbons and had a passion for climbing up towers.

Sometimes she walked with Kaspar for miles. He seemed happy in the spring as they picked flowers together. Sometimes she would twine young forest leaves in his hat which always made him look proud. One day they agreed that they should call each other Kaspar and Clara.

Size 22 ¼ x 40 ¼ inches
Acrylic & Tempera on Wood

KASPAR AND THE ANGELS

FROM *the realms above, the angels look down. Kaspar stumbles along the path of life, white clouds are forming a pathway, he is building a bridge across the spiritual divide.*

Size 16 ¼ x 13 ¼
Oil on wood

THE HOLY FOOL

IN *the chapel of the Swan Knights in the lovely Gumbertus Church; Kaspar knelt and prayed:*

"Prepare in me, oh Lord, a heart that's pure and give to me a new and steadfast spirit, cast me from thy presence not aside, nor take thy Holy Ghost away from me."

Size 19 ¾ x 17 inches
Acrylic & tempera on wood

KASPAR'S DREAM AND THE FOUNTAIN

*Together they pass chandeliers, tables and down the
corridors of time to the Fountain of Life.*

Size 13 ½ x 10 inches
Watercolour on paper

KASPAR'S DREAM AND THE CLOSED DOORS

KASPAR *had a dream. He is in a big house asleep. A woman comes in and wakes him up. He notices that the bed is so small that he does not know how he has found it large enough to lie in. The woman dresses him and leads him into a room; all around the walls are mirrors in golden frames. Behind the glass walls silver dishes are shining and on a white table there are fine, delicately-painted porcelain cups.*

He wants to remain and look about, but the woman pulls him on. There is a room with many books and from the middle of the curved ceiling a chandelier is suspended. Kaspar wants to look at the books but the lights of the chandelier slowly go out, one after the other, and the woman draws him on. She conducts him through a long corridor and down an immense staircase; they walk through a gallery in the interior of the house. He sees paintings on the walls, men in helmets and women with golden jewellery. He looks through the arch of the wall from the hall into the court where the fountain is splashing. The column of water is silver white at the bottom and at the top red with the sun.

They come to a second staircase, the steps of which mount upwards like golden clouds. An iron man is standing by the stairs, a sword in his right hand, but his face is black, no, he has no face at all. Kaspar is afraid of him and does not want to pass him, whereupon the woman bends over and whispers something in his ear. Kaspar goes by him and walks up to an immense door where the woman knocks. The door is not opened. She calls and no-one hears. She tries to open the door, but the door is locked.

Size 45½ x 16¼ inches
Acrylic & tempera on wood

100

Kaspar's Dream and the Closed Doors

Detail

PATH OF THE CROSS

KASPAR *is confronted by the great doors; the mystery of his imprisonment and death.*

Like Christ bearing the cross on Golgotha, he turns to Mary. She whispers compassionately to him as one from the stars, clothed in a deep universal blue.

Size 20 ½ x 20 ¼ inches
Acrylic & pastel on wood

THE PATH OF SACRIFICE

THE *saving boat carries Kaspar and his little horse on a journey to freedom; over the dark turbulent waters and troubled times.*

His life and suffering became a 'way of the cross', a path of sacrifice.

THE LAVENDER BAG

THE *open-hearted and innocent Kaspar was deceived by a distinguished stranger who arranged to meet Kaspar, saying he would take him to see his mother.*

As arranged Kaspar, full of hope, went to the court garden in a snowstorm to meet him. The stranger took from his pocket a small lavender bag and said to Kaspar: "Open that, inside you will find the token your mother has given us." While Kaspar tried to untie the thread around the lavender bag, the man cruelly struck Kaspar through his chest with a long sharp implement.

Size 9 x 13 inches
Gouache, wax & ink on paper

KASPAR CRAWLS IN THE SNOW

DEEPLY *wounded, Kaspar dropped the small lavender bag in the snow. Everything seemed black before his eyes; suddenly his knees gave way and he fell to the ground. He crawled along bending his head from the driving wind and snow. He called out "Ducatus, Ducatus".*

Kaspar Hauser died on the evening of Tuesday 17th December 1883. His final words were full of thankfulness towards his friends, and forgiveness towards anyone who had harmed him.

Size 12 x 9 ½ inches
Gouache & wax on paper

MURDERERS

CLARA *made her way to the cemetery to see the grave of Kaspar Hauser. Two workmen had just leaned a cross against a weeping willow tree by his grave. They fastened to the cross a heart-shaped shield with the words on it:*

> *Here lies Kaspar Hauser*
> *A riddle for his age*
> *His origin unknown*
> *A mystery his death*

They then placed it at the head of the grave. As the clergyman and the other people assembled around the grave, Clara suddenly turned on them, shouting aloud: "You are all murderers, murderers, murderers."

Size 14 ½ x 12 ½ inches
Gouache & wax on paper

Murderers

Detail - Clara

KASPAR JONAH

Kaspar, entering into Death, descends like Jonah to the bottom of the waters, to the bottom of the world.

Size 9 x 10 ¾ inches
Oil on Wood

THE SAVING OF KASPAR HAUSER

Kaspar like Jonah lies on the shore of the new land.
He is raised up in the realms of spirit.

Size 9 x 10¾ inches
Oil on Wood

THE PASSING OF KASPAR HAUSER

"Father, not my, but thy will be done."

Kaspar Hauser

Size 37 ¾ x 33 ¾ inches
Tempera & acrylic on wood

THE ARK BEARER

Kaspar, like Noah, carries the Ark with the precious seeds of life across the flood; the apocalyptic waters of destruction.

Size 9 x 10 ¾ inches
Oil on wood

Moses, Kaspar and the Tablets

THE *seeds of life are saved. The sheaths enshroud the new-born life. Moses in the bulrushes is saved to lead a nation from captivity. Kaspar's life works into the world as a saving seed; to raise mankind from captivity.*

Size 9 x 10¾ inches
Oil on wood

MOSES, KASPAR AND THE TABLETS

Detail - Moses

THE PASSING OVER

With *a guiding hand Kaspar embraces the community of souls led by Christ. They move together in the Ark Boat across troubled waters, through the ages.*

Size 9 x 10¾ inches
Oil on wood

The Kingdom of Kaspar Hauser

ON the princely carriage Kaspar and the little horse enter a beautiful kingdom. The Holy Fool on the path of the Grail awakens in us a world of community, beauty and light.

Size 19 ¾ x 18 inches
Oil on Wood

THE KINGDOM OF KASPAR HAUSER

Detail

Appendix To The Paintings

HERE is a thread that runs through much of Greg Tricker's work. A theme which is continually developed, nurtured and matured; this is the image of 'The Innocent in the world'. When I first met Greg in 1989 he had just completed a series of batik paintings that celebrated the life and death of Anne Frank. Wise beyond her years, her courageous spirit lit a beacon of conscience, in an otherwise very dark world. These batik paintings were exhibited at Ruskin Mill, St Clement Danes, London and several cathedrals throughout England. A little book of these paintings was complemented by the poems of Nick Naydler and published in 1991.

His next great body of work derived its inspiration from Catacomb Art and a visit to Rome and appeared in book form in 2002. Here wise/innocence is not so much expressed by an individual human victim as by the nature of early Christianity, shown like a radiant seed in a decaying and power hungry world.

The St Francis paintings and sculptures, a series of work completed in 2004 and appearing in book form in 2005, begin to touch on a quality which becomes central to the Kaspar Hauser work. This is the quality of sacred foolishness, the Fool as Holy Man. The acts of St. Francis were unworldly foolish, opposed to all that is comfortable, complacent and self-interested, they were rather the expressions of unconditional longing for union with the Godhead. The paintings were exhibited at Salisbury Cathedral and Piano Nobile Gallery, London in 2005.

In the Kaspar Hauser paintings, the theme of 'The Innocent in the world', reaches its zenith. Kaspar is the victim of the forces that stand in opposition to the true, sacred, inner kernel of man. That, which despite long experience and the gradual descent into the material world, has retained its link to the spirit, is still fresh and pure and foolish. Greg Tricker's paintings are both illustrative and evocative. They tell a 'story', but through the images a much greater tale is told. The paintings stand in that creative space which is neither naturalistic nor abstract, where the imagination of the viewer needs to apply itself to a process of understanding and empathy. This middle sphere of the imagination and the understanding heart, is what Greg Tricker works out of. His pictures are born out of a simplicity, a sense of the real; but above all they are direct expressions of that which is felt, imagined and intuited. To the extent that egotism and self-will departs from the work, the artist becomes a messenger inspired by angelic promptings that touch upon the Universally Real.

The Seven Themes of the Paintings

The Kaspar Hauser paintings can be loosely divided into seven great themes; the first shows Kaspar's early imprisonment. These paintings evoke a sense of great loneliness and isolation which the toy horses seem to enhance rather than mitigate. In *The Horses* (page 51) and in *My Friend* (page 55), the image is created almost in monochrome, the outline scratched into the surface. It brings to mind a cave painting or the sort of spontaneous pictures that a prisoner might scratch onto his cell wall with a nail.

The second theme concerns itself with Kaspar's appearance; innocence is confronted by the world. This is well represented by the painting called *The Theatre of the World* (page 65). Unsteadily, clutching his letter and his sun like hat, Kaspar makes his appearance. One is reminded of the Grimm's hero 'Lucky Hans' whose wages for seven years hard work is a lump of gold the size of his head. The 'foolish' Hans, exchanges it for ever diminishing returns until finally he owns an ordinary boulder which falls into a well. Thus he earns nothing for his pains, but is cheerful, free and unburdened. In the painting the curtains are drawn aside, the audience representing mankind watches intently and like the snake in paradise, the black pantomime figure intimates menace, perhaps even suggests death.

This theatre aspect is continued in the third theme, that of Greek tragedy. Something is acted out on the stage of life, which is at once poignant, intimate and yet infinitely remote. Greek actors wore masks and in the painting called *The Mystery of Kaspar Hauser* (page 53) and in the *Water of Life* (page 41), Kaspar's face has a mask-like quality. The secret of Kaspar's life is hidden and the tragedy of that which is to come, already implied, foreshadowed.

The painting entitled *The Circus Life* (plate 87) defines the fourth theme. Kaspar stares uncomprehendingly up at Frau Biberbach who has just evicted him from her house. His life was a kind of balancing act on a high wire, but here the woman is shown high up near the roof of the big top in a kind of crow's nest, her actions are 'risky' and 'dangerous' but ultimately only endanger herself. Kaspar is dressed in a Harlequin outfit and one is reminded of Picasso's many pictures of Harlequins and acrobats. They represent a fascinating homeless outsider class, wandering creatures of the circus, beings beyond the norm of society. In this sense Kaspar is a vagrant, a homeless wanderer, entertaining for a while the heartless world with his simplicity.

The fifth theme of the Holy Fool is really central to the whole work. The paintings *The Paradise Garden* page 77) and *The Holy Fool* (page 97) defines this theme. In both, Kaspar wears a tall crown-like hat which is reminiscent of a jester's cap, a dunce hat and a Bishop's mitre. He represents that untouched and untouchable aspect of the inner man, sacred, forever innocent and foolish in the eyes of the world. With the Sacred Fool theme, Greg taps into a current of English Art that has its roots both in William Blake and in Cecil Collins. Blake turned his back on the 'dark satanic mills' of the Industrial Revolution and celebrated the innocence of nature, for Collins 'the Fool' represented the highest ideal of human striving, the very Christ Himself.

The sixth theme, Kaspar's path of sacrifice is represented in the paintings *The Path of the Cross* (page 105) and *The Path of Sacrifice* (page 107). *The Passing of Kaspar Hauser* (page 121) also strongly belongs to this series but begins to resonate with another subtle quality. *The Path of the Cross* is an echo of Christ's path of suffering, his way of calvary. A female figure, possibly Mary, reassures and comforts him. In the painting *The Path of Sacrifice* Kaspar is shown as a cross bearer, in as much as he bears both his own suffering and the pain of the world. In *The Passing of Kaspar Hauser* the dying boy, surrounded by his toys and the paraphernalia of life, at one and the same time awaits death, but is already resurrected. A quiet luminosity shines from his body and death has lost its sting.

The seventh theme, paintings all done towards the end of Greg's Kaspar Hauser work, extend themselves into the archetypal and the universal. The pictures are all quite small and with the exception of the painting *The Kingdom of Kaspar Hauser* (page 131), emerge out of darkness. This painting in gold, turquoise and black is both transcendental and shows an ever present state, in which the Sacred Fool has become the Eternal King. In the painting *Kaspar the Ark Bearer* (page 123), Kaspar is shown holding The Ark in his hand, carrying it like a precious box across the flood. In this sense he is the preserver of all those truly human qualities that lead into the future.

Kaspar Jonah (page 117), takes up the theme of initiation sleep, an idea that Greg has worked with for many years. Kaspar's imprisonment and release was a kind of initiation; on one level perhaps his whole earthly life was a descent into the belly of the whale. *Kaspar and The Lions* (page 47), seems to explore his nature as pure spirit untouched and unmolested by the devouring world. The wild beasts sent to tear him limb from limb become tranquil in the presence of the Holy Fool—'The Lion lies down with the Lamb'. *Moses, Kaspar and the Tablets* (page 125) perhaps touches on the development of a new morality. Moses gave the law, inscribed into the very stone itself; Kaspar teaches us 'conscience'. This conscience is as yet a tender being, a child in a basket, rocked by the oceans of the world. In the painting entitled *The Saving of Kaspar Hauser* (page 119), Kaspar now in the form of a winged seraph is carried by a God-like figure, ancient and bearded, reminiscent of the work of Blake. *Kaspar and the Angels* (page 95) belongs very definitely to this series. Kaspar wanders through the 'hills and vales' of earth life, watched over by the angels. Behind him is a shimmering trail of cloud, a bridge between the heavenly waters and those of earth.

The images of this final series emerge out of darkness, out of 'night', as it were. Night in this sense is not the absence of light, but a spiritual state. Waves and clouds have become flat, linear and ever repeating. One hears something of the eternal rush of the ocean in these paintings, the Sea of the Soul, infinitely beats against the Shore of our Hearts.

Johannes Steuck

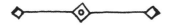

ACKNOWLEDGEMENT

OVER the years many hundreds of books have been written about Kaspar Hauser. I would like to acknowledge the particular inspiration of two people; Jacob Wassermann and Rudolf Steiner. In his novel, *Caspar Hauser, Enigma of a Century*, Wassermann creates a very full, subtle and richly woven portrait of Kaspar. Although some of the components of this portrait are 'imaginative' it extends effortlessly into a realm of spiritual truths. Through Rudolf Steiner these truths are taken onto another level and an instinct for integrity becomes a knowledge of truth. Rudolf Steiner (1861–1925) was the pioneer of a new kind of research, a research which combined the fruits of rational thinking with a deep insight into the spiritual world. In so far as I have drawn creative inspiration from Rudolf Steiner's insights, he stands as a kind of Godfather to this text. All quoted material throughout the text can be referenced from the bibliography.

Kaspar Hauser—A Life Obscured
is dedicated to my parents
Lisa and Udo Steuck

Johannes Steuck 2006

Selected Bibliography

Caspar Hauser: The Enigma of a century
Jacob Wassermann, Floris Classics.
ISBN 0-86315-505-7

Kaspar Hauser: The Struggle for the Spirit
Peter Tradowsky, Temple Lodge.
ISBN 0-904693-89-9

Who was Kaspar Hauser?
An essay and a play by Carlo Pietzner, Floris Books.

Kaspar Hauser speaks for himself
Camphill Books.

The Christmas Story
Karl König, Camphill Books.

Kaspar Hauser: Das Kind von Europa
Peter Tradowsky, Urachhaus.

The First Three Years of the Child
Karl König, Anthroposophic Press.

Songs of Innocence and of Experience
William Blake, Oxford Paperbacks.

Voyage of the Dawn Treader
C.S. Lewis, Puffin Books.

From Jesus to Christ
Rudolf Steiner Press.

Esoteric Christianity and the Mission of Christian Rosenkreutz
Rudolf Steiner Press.

The Vision of the Fool & Other Writings
Cecil Collins, Golgonooza Press
ISBN 0-903880-75-X

Secret Brotherhoods
Rudolf Steiner Press.

We acknowledge with thanks limited use of quotations from the above books.

GENEALOGICAL TABLE

1. Grand Duke of Baden

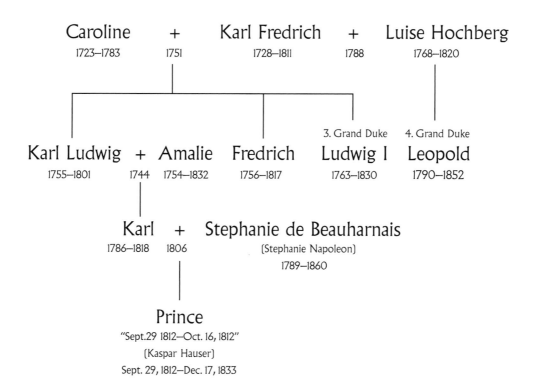

Caroline   +   Karl Fredrich   +   Luise Hochberg
1723–1783   1751   1728–1811   1788   1768–1820

3. Grand Duke   4. Grand Duke

Karl Ludwig   +   Amalie   Fredrich   Ludwig I   Leopold
1755–1801   1744   1754–1832   1756–1817   1763–1830   1790–1852

Karl   +   Stephanie de Beauharnais
1786–1818   1806   (Stephanie Napoleon)
1789–1860

Prince
"Sept.29 1812–Oct. 16, 1812"
(Kaspar Hauser)
Sept. 29, 1812–Dec. 17, 1833

OTHER BOOKS BY GREG TRICKER

Francis of Assisi–Paintings For Our Time
Paintings by Greg Tricker, Text by Johannes Steuck
Green books; Tel: 01803 863260
Gloucestershire 2005
ISBN 903998-66-2
Format 330 x 221mm x 60 colour plates; Price £25.00
Hard Bound.
£25.00

This inspired collection of over sixty original paintings, stone carvings and woodcut prints by Greg Tricker portrays the human suffering, exultation, compassion and joy of the life of St Francis; with their visionary quality, they present a fresh, contemporary image of St Francis.

Greg Tricker travelled to Assisi to research St Francis, drawing inspiration from the small church of San Damiano where the saint prayed and the square of San Rufino where he preached; and by walking through the beautiful olive groves and hills that surround Assisi.

The plates are complemented by a lively text on the historical background and life of St Francis by artist and teacher Johannes Steuck, and a spirited introduction by writer and philosopher Jeremy Naydler.

The following books are available from Greg Tricker at:
The Cottage, Millbottom, Nailsworth, GLOS GL6 0LA
Tel: 01453 834975

The Catacombs
Paintings by Greg Tricker, Text by Johannes Steuck
21 Colour Plates; Format 250 X 290mm
Gloucestershire 2002
The paintings and stone carvings are centred around early Christianity
and are inspired by the wall paintings in the catacombs, the ancient
Christian burial chambers found beneath Rome dating from 1st–3rd century AD
£17.50

For Anne Frank
21 Colour Plates; Format 215 X 150mm
With poems by Nick Naydler
Bristol 1991
£7.00

For Alice Rose
11 Colour Etchings and 10 Line Drawings
With poems by Nick Naydler
£8.50 + p&p